HAL LEONARD
BASS
TAB METHOD

BOOK ONE

Written by Eric W. Wills

Contributing Editors: Kurt Plahna, Jeff Schroedl, and Jim Schustedt

To access audio visit:
www.halleonard.com/mylibrary

Enter Code
3845-6654-8293-8724

ISBN 978-1-4768-9972-5

7777 W. BLUEMOUND RD. P.O. BOX 13819 MILWAUKEE, WI 53213

Copyright © 2013 by HAL LEONARD CORPORATION
International Copyright Secured   All Rights Reserved

For all works contained herein: Unauthorized copying, arranging, adapting, recording, Internet posting, public performance,
or other distribution of the printed or recorded music in this publication is an infringement of copyright. Infringers are liable under the law.

Visit Hal Leonard Online at
www.halleonard.com

GETTING STARTED

PARTS OF THE BASS GUITAR

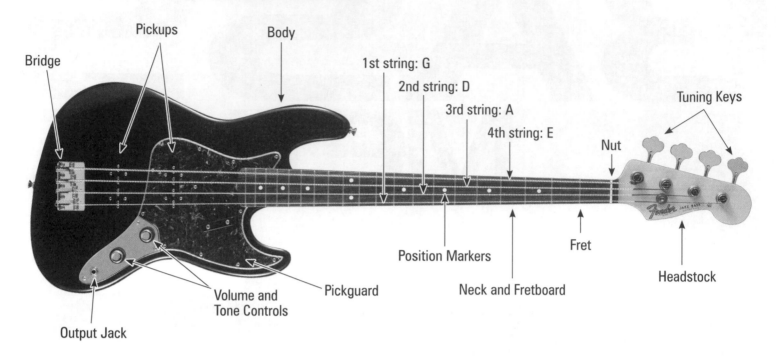

Bridge

Pickups

Body

1st string: G

2nd string: D

3rd string: A

4th string: E

Tuning Keys

Nut

Fret

Position Markers

Neck and Fretboard

Headstock

Pickguard

Volume and Tone Controls

Output Jack

THE BASS AMP

To hear yourself clearly, it is necessary to play the electric bass through an amplifier. Amps come in a wide range of sizes, but a simple, small unit like the one pictured here will work well. With the amplifier off, plug one end of an instrument cable, or "patch cord," into the bass and the other end into the input jack on the amp. Next, make sure the amp's volume is all the way down and the tone controls are set at 12 o'clock. Now turn the unit on and slowly raise the volume knob while plucking an open string until the right volume level is achieved.

TUNING

The quickest and most accurate way to get in tune is to use an electronic tuner. The four open strings on a bass should be tuned to these pitches:

E (thickest)–A–D–G (thinnest)

To tune your bass, adjust the tuning keys on the headstock. Tightening a key will raise the pitch of a string; loosening a key will lower the pitch. It's important to turn the keys slowly so that you don't overshoot your mark.

After plugging in to the tuner, make sure the volume control on the bass is turned (clockwise) all the way up. Starting with the high G, strike the open string and adjust the tuning key until the tuner's meter indicates that the pitch is correct. Follow the same process with the D, A, and E strings. Or, listen to each string's correct pitch on track 1 and turn the tuning key until the sound of the string matches the sound on the track.

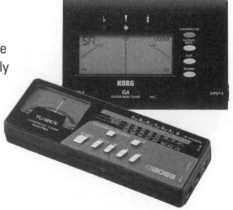

HOLDING THE BASS

Use the pictures below to help find a comfortable playing position. Whether you decide to sit or stand, it's important to remain relaxed and tension-free.

LEFT-HAND POSITION

Fingers are numbered 1 through 4. Arch your fingers and press the strings down firmly between the frets with your fingertips only.

Place your thumb on the underside of the bass guitar neck. Avoid letting the palm of your hand touch the neck.

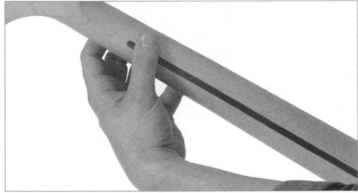

RIGHT-HAND POSITION

Rest your thumb on top of the pickup of the bass and let your fingers hang down loosely over the strings. Use your index and middle fingers alternately to pluck the strings upward, coming to rest on your thumb.

THE E STRING

Bass guitar music is written in a form of notation called **tablature**, or **tab** for short. Each horizontal line represents a string, and each number represents a fret. The thickest string played open, or not pressed, is the low E note. In tab, an open string is represented with a zero (0). The note F is located on the 1st fret. Press, or "fret" the string with your 1st finger, directly behind the first metal fret.

GETTING THE FEEL 2»

Begin by playing only open E notes. Place the pad of your picking-hand index finger on the E string, press down lightly, and drag it across to your thumb, allowing the string to ring out. Next, use your middle finger to pluck the string in the same fashion. Continue to alternate between these two fingers until it feels natural.

THEME FROM "JAWS" 3»

Play the theme from the movie *Jaws* using the notes E and F. To get a good sound from the F, make sure your 1st finger presses down just behind (not on top of) the 1st fret. Alternate your picking fingers as in the last exercise. Speed up as the numbers get closer together.

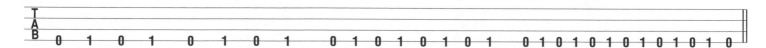

By John Williams
Copyright © 1975 USI B MUSIC PUBLISHING
Copyright Renewed
All Rights Controlled and Administered by SONGS OF UNIVERSAL, INC

Now let's learn more notes on the E string.

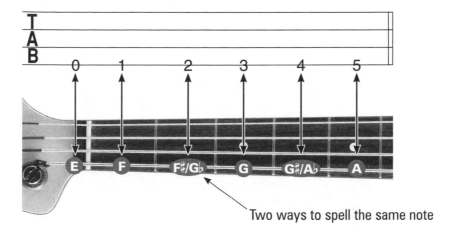

Two ways to spell the same note

GREEN ONIONS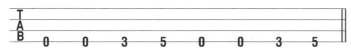

"Green Onions" by Booker T. & the MG's uses the notes E, G, and A. Follow the tab and play the notes at a steady speed, or **tempo**. Use your 1st finger to fret the G note and 4th finger to fret the A.

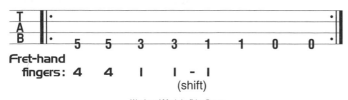

Written by Al Jackson, Jr., Lewis Steinberg, Booker T. Jones and Steve Cropper
© 1962 (Renewed 1990) AL JACKSON JR. MUSIC (BMI) and IRVING MUSIC, INC.
All Rights for AL JACKSON JR. MUSIC Administered by BUG MUSIC, INC., a BMG CHRYSALIS company

MY GENERATION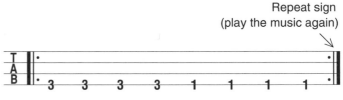

"My Generation" by the Who begins with this two-note phrase. Use your 1st finger to fret F and 4th finger for G. The **repeat signs** tell you to play the music again. Practice this example slowly and steadily at first before increasing the tempo.

Repeat sign
(play the music again)

Words and Music by Peter Townshend
© Copyright 1965 (Renewed) Fabulous Music Ltd., London, England
TRO - Devon Music, Inc., New York, controls all publication rights for the U.S.A. and Canada

STRAY CAT STRUT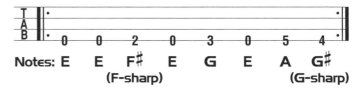

Besides the famous song by the Stray Cats, this bass line has been used in many tunes. "Hit the Road Jack" by Ray Charles is one example. Begin with your 4th finger on A. After playing the second G note with your 1st finger, you'll have to shift your fret hand down to play the F with your 1st finger.

Fret-hand
fingers: 4   4   1   1 - 1
                         (shift)

Words and Music by Brian Setzer
© 1981 EMI LONGITUDE MUSIC and ROCKIN' BONES MUSIC
All Rights Controlled and Administered by EMI LONGITUDE MUSIC

PETER GUNN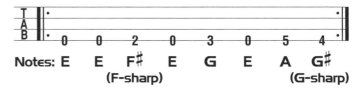

A **riff** is a short, composed phrase that is repeated. The popular riff from "Peter Gunn" is played with notes on the low E string.

Notes: E   E   F#   E   G   E   A   G#
              (F-sharp)   (G-sharp)

By Henry Mancini
Copyright © 1958 NORTHRIDGE MUSIC CO.
Copyright Renewed
All Rights Controlled and Administered by UNIVERSAL MUSIC CORP.

FOR WHOM THE BELL TOLLS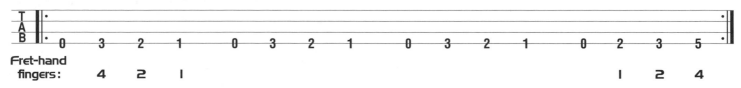

Whenever you play a span of three consecutive frets on the lower portion of the bass neck (first five frets), use only your 1st, 2nd, and 4th fret-hand fingers. Skipping the 3rd finger will limit tension in your hand and wrist.

Fret-hand
fingers: 4   2   1   1   2   4

Words and Music by James Hetfield, Lars Ulrich and Cliff Burton
Copyright © 1984 Creeping Death Music (ASCAP)

THE A STRING

Here are the notes within the first five frets of the 3rd string, called the A string.

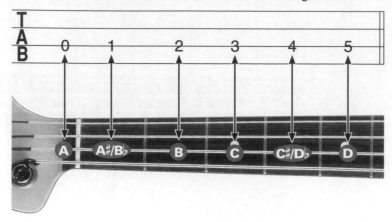

BRIT ROCK

This catchy riff uses the notes A, B, and C. To get the best sound from any note on the A string, pluck the string, letting your picking finger come to rest against the E string.

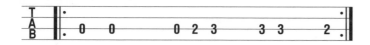

Copyright © 2012 by HAL LEONARD CORPORATION

LEAN ON ME

This song was a #1 hit in two decades. It uses the notes A, B, C#, and D. There are a few correct ways to finger this riff with your fret hand, but the one written below works well with minimal hand strain.

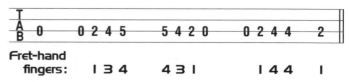

Fret-hand
fingers: 1 3 4   4 3 1   1 4 4   1

Words and Music by Bill Withers
Copyright © 1972 INTERIOR MUSIC CORP.
Copyright Renewed
All Rights Controlled and Administered by SONGS OF UNIVERSAL, INC.

RHYTHM TAB

Rhythm tab adds rhythmic values to the basic tab staff. **Bar lines** divide music into **measures**. A **time signature** tells how many beats are in each measure and what kind of note is counted as one beat. In 4/4 time ("four-four"), there are four beats in each measure, and a **quarter note** is counted as one beat. It has a vertical stem joined to the tab number.

FEEL THE BEAT

Count "1, 2, 3, 4" as you play.

Quarter-note stem

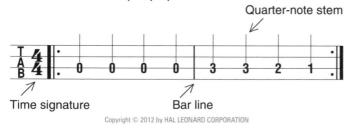

Time signature   Bar line

Copyright © 2012 by HAL LEONARD CORPORATION

LADY MADONNA

This classic riff by the Beatles uses quarter notes on strings 3 and 4.

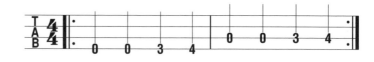

Words and Music by John Lennon and Paul McCartney
Copyright © 1968 Sony/ATV Music Publishing LLC
Copyright Renewed
All Rights Administered by Sony/ATV Music Publishing LLC, 8 Music Square West, Nashville, TN 37203

ZEPPELIN TRIBUTE

Make sure your thumb is anchored on the pickup for picking-hand stability.

BLUES RIFF

Moving from B with your 1st finger to C# with your 3rd can be a bit of a stretch for your hand. To minimize strain, quickly shift your hand up the neck after playing B to get in position for the following note.

Fret-hand
fingers: 4   1   3   4   3   1   4

Copyright © 2012 by HAL LEONARD CORPORATION   Copyright © 2012 by HAL LEONARD CORPORATION

MORE RIFFS

The next two riffs are written in **3/4 time**. This means there are three beats in each measure, and a quarter note receives one beat.

MY NAME IS JONAS

Count "1–2–3, 1–2–3" as you play this riff by the band Weezer.

Words and Music by Rivers Cuomo, Patrick Wilson and Jason Cropper
Copyright © 1994 E.O. Smith Music, Fie! and Ubermommasuprapoppa Music
All Rights for E.O. Smith Music and Fie! Administered by Wixen Music Publishing, Inc.

MALAGUEÑA

This traditional Spanish piece is very popular among classical guitarists.

By Francisco Tarrega
Copyright © 2013 by HAL LEONARD CORPORATION

A **half note** lasts two beats. It fills the time of two quarter notes. In tab, a circle surrounds the tab number(s) and is attached to a vertical stem.

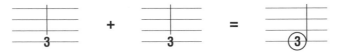

CANON IN D

The first line is played with half notes and the second line is played with quarter notes. Count aloud and keep a steady tempo.

Count: one (two) three (four) etc.

By Johann Pachelbel
Copyright © 2013 by HAL LEONARD CORPORATION

ELECTRIC FUNERAL

The heavy metal band Black Sabbath used half notes and quarter notes for this powerful, eerie riff.

Words and Music by Frank Iommi, John Osbourne, William Ward and Terence Butler
© Copyright 1970 (Renewed) and 1974 (Renewed) Onward Music Ltd., London, England
TRO - Essex Music International, Inc., New York, controls all publication rights for the U.S.A. and Canada

ALL BLUES

Now try playing half notes in 3/4 time.

By Miles Davis
Copyright © 1959 JAZZ HORN MUSIC CORP.
Copyright Renewed
All Rights Controlled and Administered by SONGS OF UNIVERSAL, INC.

An **eighth note** lasts half a beat, or half as long as a quarter note. One eighth note is written with a stem and flag; consecutive eighth notes are connected with a beam.

WITH OR WITHOUT YOU 20))

This classic song by U2 has a repetitive, eighth-note bass line. When counting eighth notes, use the word "and" between the beats—1 and 2 and 3 and 4 and. The numbers are called **downbeats** and each "and" is called an **upbeat**.

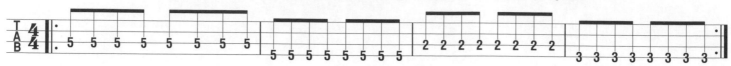

Count: one and two and three and four and

Words and Music by U2
Copyright © 1987 UNIVERSAL MUSIC PUBLISHING INTERNATIONAL B.V.
All Rights in the United States and Canada Controlled and Administered by UNIVERSAL - POLYGRAM INTERNATIONAL PUBLISHING, INC.

AQUALUNG 21))

Now let's mix eighth notes and quarter notes on this famous Jethro Tull song.

Words and Music by Ian Anderson and Jennie Anderson
Copyright © 1971 The Ian Anderson Group Of Companies Ltd.
Copyright Renewed
All Rights Administered by Chrysalis Music Group Inc., a BMG Chrysalis company

GREEN-EYED LADY 22))

Experiment to determine which fingers work best for this classic Sugarloaf riff.

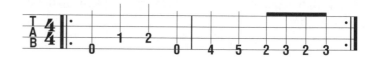

Words and Music by Jerry Corbetta, J.C. Phillips and David Riordan
© 1970 (Renewed) CLARIDGE MUSIC COMPANY, A Division of MPL Music Publishing, Inc.

A **rest** is a symbol used to indicate silence in music. In 4/4 time, a **quarter rest** fills the time of one beat and a **half rest** fills the time of two beats.

Quarter Rest
One Beat

Half Rest
Two Beats

25 OR 6 TO 4 23))

This riff by the band Chicago uses a quarter rest. Mute the string by touching it with the tip of your picking finger. You can also release the pressure of your fret hand to silence the string.

Count: one and two and three (four)

Words and Music by Robert Lamm
Copyright © 1970 Primary Wave Lamm, Aurelius Music and Spirit Catalog Holdings, S.à.r.l.
Copyright Renewed
All Rights for Aurelius Music Controlled and Administered throughout the world by Spirit Two Music, Inc.
All Rights for Spirit Catalog Holdings, S.à.r.l. Controlled and Administered in the U.S., Canada, UK and Eire by Spirit Two Music, Inc.
All Rights for Spirit Catalog Holdings, S.à.r.l. Controlled and Administered throughout the world excluding the U.S., Canada, UK and Eire by Spirit Services Holdings S.à.r.l.

BRAIN STEW 24))

The band Green Day used a similar descending pattern for this hit song, which uses quarter and half rests.

Count: one and (two) (three - four)

from the TriStar Motion Picture GODZILLA (The Godzilla Remix)
Words by Billie Joe
Music by Green Day
Copyright © 1995, 1996, 1998 TSP Music, Inc., WB Music Corp. and Green Daze Music
All Rights on behalf of TSP Music, Inc. Administered by Sony/ATV Music Publishing LLC, 8 Music Square West, Nashville, TN 37203
All Rights on behalf of Green Daze Music Administered by WB Music Corp.

THE D STRING

Here are the notes within the first five frets of the 2nd string, called the D string.

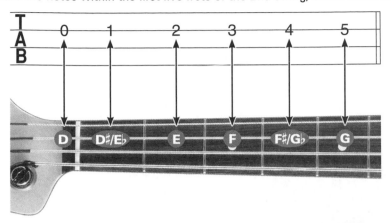

D-MENTED

When playing multiple notes on the D string, you should move your picking-hand thumb, which was resting on the pickup, to the E string as pictured to the right. This move will help you to reach the D string more easily with your picking fingers. Say the notes out loud as you play this riff.

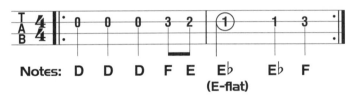

Notes: D D D F E E♭   E♭ F
                        (E-flat)

Copyright © 2012 by HAL LEONARD CORPORATION

MACHINE GUN

Jimi Hendrix used this riff as the foundation for his song from the album *Band of Gypsys*.

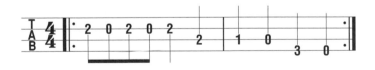

Words and Music by Jimi Hendrix
Copyright © 1970 by EXPERIENCE HENDRIX, L.L.C.
Copyright Renewed 1998
All Rights Controlled and Administered by EXPERIENCE HENDRIX, L.L.C.

BILLIE JEAN

Notice the fret-hand fingering from F♯ to C♯ in this Michael Jackson hit. The transition from a higher to lower string on the same fret can be made smoother by using two fingers as written here. Rest your thumb on the E string throughout this riff.

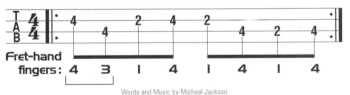

Fret-hand
fingers: 4 3 1 4 1 4 1 4

Words and Music by Michael Jackson
Copyright © 1982 Mijac Music
All Rights Administered by Sony/ATV Music Publishing LLC, 8 Music Square West, Nashville, TN 37203

YOU GIVE LOVE A BAD NAME

Use the same type of fingering pattern across the A and E strings here that you did in "Billie Jean."

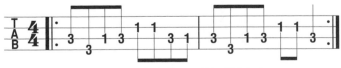

Words and Music by Jon Bon Jovi, Desmond Child and Richie Sambora
Copyright © 1986 UNIVERSAL - POLYGRAM INTERNATIONAL PUBLISHING, INC., BON JOVI PUBLISHING,
SONY/ATV MUSIC PUBLISHING LLC and AGGRESSIVE MUSIC
All Rights for BON JOVI PUBLISHING Controlled and Administered by UNIVERSAL -
POLYGRAM INTERNATIONAL PUBLISHING, INC.
All Rights for SONY/ATV MUSIC PUBLISHING LLC and AGGRESSIVE MUSIC Administered by SONY/ATV MUSIC
PUBLISHING LLC, 8 Music Square West, Nashville, TN 37203

AUTHORITY SONG

Begin with your picking-hand thumb resting on the E string to play the notes on the D string. Then shift your thumb to the pickup for the rest of the riff. Skipping the A string makes this bass line tricky, so practice slowly.

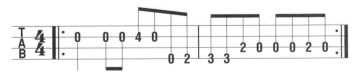

Words and Music by John Mellencamp
© 1983 EMI FULL KEEL MUSIC

A **tie** is a curved, dashed line connecting two notes of the same pitch. It tells you not to strike the second note. The first note should be struck and held for the combined value of both notes.

Two Beats   Three Beats   One Beat

TIE IT DOWN
The tie in this riff connects a quarter note on beat 4 to a quarter note on beat 1 of the next measure. Count as you play.

Copyright © 2013 by HAL LEONARD CORPORATION

I HEARD IT THROUGH THE GRAPEVINE
There are two different ties in this Motown bass riff. The second one that happens ties the "and" of beat 3 to beat 4, lasting one and a half beats total. Listen to the audio example for reference.

Words and Music by Norman J. Whitfield and Barrett Strong
© 1966 (Renewed 1994) JOBETE MUSIC CO., INC.
All Rights Controlled and Administered by EMI BLACKWOOD MUSIC INC. on behalf of STONE AGATE MUSIC
(A Division of JOBETE MUSIC CO., INC.)

(SITTIN' ON) THE DOCK OF THE BAY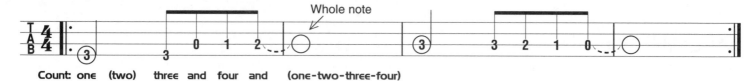
This recognizable bass line from Otis Redding's #1 hit song connects the last eighth note of one measure to a **whole note** in the following measure. A whole note lasts four beats.

Words and Music by Steve Cropper and Otis Redding
Copyright © 1968, 1975 IRVING MUSIC, INC.
Copyright Renewed
All Rights for the world outside the U.S. Controlled and Administered by WB MUSIC CORP. and IRVING MUSIC INC.

SPACE TRUCKIN'
You're now ready to tackle this driving bass line from the band Deep Purple. After repeating the first two measures, try to continue on to the next without missing a beat.

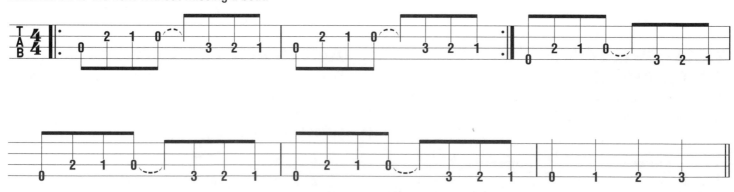

Words and Music by Ritchie Blackmore, Ian Gillan, Roger Glover, Jon Lord and Ian Paice
© 1972 (Renewed 2000) B. FELDMAN & CO. LTD. trading as HEC MUSIC
All Rights for the United States and Canada Controlled and Administered by GLENWOOD MUSIC CORP.

An **eighth rest** indicates to be silent for half a beat. It looks like this: ⅞

HAVA NAGILA (LET'S BE HAPPY)

Start slowly and use your pinky for the G♯ on the 4th fret.

Count: one two (three) and four and

Lyrics by Moshe Nathanson
Music by Abraham Z. Idelsohn
Copyright © 2013 by HAL LEONARD CORPORATION

PORK AND BEANS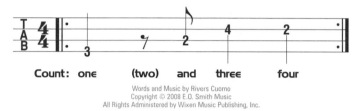

This repeating riff is a prominent part in one of Weezer's biggest hits.

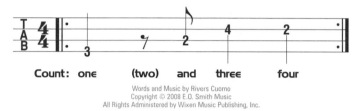

Count: one (two) and three four

Words and Music by Rivers Cuomo
Copyright © 2008 E.O. Smith Music
All Rights Administered by Wixen Music Publishing, Inc.

CROSSFIRE

The legendary Stevie Ray Vaughan recorded this song which is anchored by a hard-hitting bass line.

Words and Music by Bill Carter, Ruth Ellsworth, Reese Wynans, Tommy Shannon and Chris Layton
© 1989 BLAME MUSIC (BMI) and MANCHACA MUSIC (BMI)/Administered by BUG MUSIC, INC.,
a BMG CHRYSALIS COMPANY

A **staccato** mark looks like a dot written above or below a note. It indicates that the note it is attached to should be played shorter than normal, and can be an important component to the feel of a bass line.

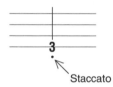

Staccato

SUPER FREAK

This funky Rick James hit uses both eighth and quarter rests.

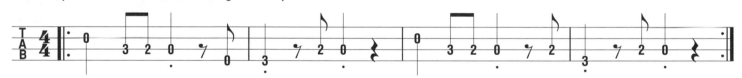

Words and Music by Rick James and Alonzo Miller
© 1981 JOBETE MUSIC CO., INC. and STONE DIAMOND MUSIC CORP.
All Rights Controlled and Administered by EMI APRIL MUSIC INC. and EMI BLACKWOOD MUSIC INC.

PUMP IT UP

Here's the intro riff to a song by Elvis Costello. To get the staccato notes short, release the pressure of your fret hand from the note, as you would for a rest.

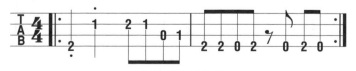

Words and Music by Elvis Costello
Copyright © 1978 by Universal Music Publishing MGB Ltd.
All Rights in the United States and Canada Administered by Universal Music - MGB Songs

LOUIE, LOUIE

Use your fret hand to stop the sound of an open string for a rest or staccato note by lightly placing it on top of the strings.

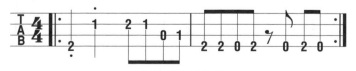

Words and Music by Richard Berry
© 1957 (Renewed 1985) EMI LONGITUDE MUSIC

A special technique for the fret hand is the **finger roll**. This is helpful when you need to quickly and smoothly move between two notes on adjacent strings that are on the same fret. To do this when moving from a lower to a higher string, play the note on the lower string with the tip of your finger and your knuckle slightly bent [Photo 1]. Then flatten the knuckle and roll your finger to the next string, playing the note on the higher string with the pad of your finger [Photo 2]. Reverse the sequence when rolling from a higher to a lower string.

Photo 1

Photo 2

DAY TRIPPER 40

On this Beatles classic, roll from the 3rd to the 2nd string using your index finger.

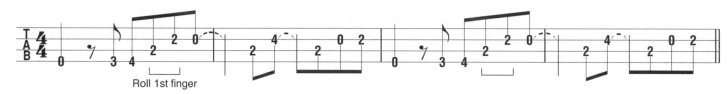

Roll 1st finger

Words and Music by John Lennon and Paul McCartney
Copyright © 1965 Sony/ATV Music Publishing LLC
Copyright Renewed
All Rights Administered by Sony/ATV Music Publishing LLC, 8 Music Square West, Nashville, TN 37203

JAZZY 41

Begin this jazz-style bass line with your 4th finger on the third fret. Then use your 2nd finger to roll across the two notes on the second fret.

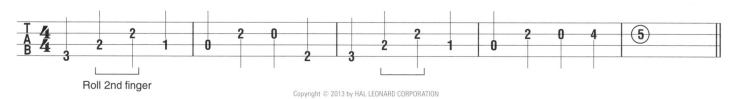

Roll 2nd finger

Copyright © 2013 by HAL LEONARD CORPORATION

The next riffs begin with **pickup notes**. Count pickup notes as if they were the last portion of a full measure.

YOU REALLY GOT ME 42

Van Halen covered this Kinks song on their first album.

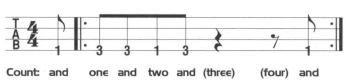

Count: and   one and two and (three) (four) and

Words and Music by Ray Davies
Copyright © 1964 Jayboy Music Corp.
Copyright Renewed
All Rights Administered by Sony/ATV Music Publishing LLC, 8 Music Square West, Nashville, TN 37203

MISSISSIPPI QUEEN 43

The intro to this song by the band Mountain has a one-and-a-half beat pickup.

Count: and four and   one

Words and Music by Leslie West, Felix Pappalardi, Corky Laing and David Rea
Copyright © 1970 by Universal Music - MGB Songs
Copyright Renewed

ALL THE SMALL THINGS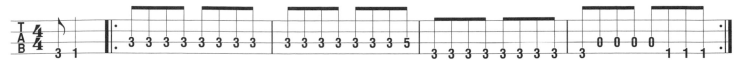

This song by Blink-182 opens with a fast, driving bass line. Play the C notes with your 1st finger so you can reach the D with your 4th.

Words and Music by Tom De Longe and Mark Hoppus
© 1999 EMI APRIL MUSIC INC. and FUN WITH GOATS
All Rights Controlled and Administered by EMI APRIL MUSIC INC.

I WALK THE LINE

There's a three-beat pickup in the intro to this famous Johnny Cash song. The **fermata** sign above the last note of the song tells you to hold the note longer than its normal value to create a nice ending. Fermatas are also used within songs to create a pause in the music.

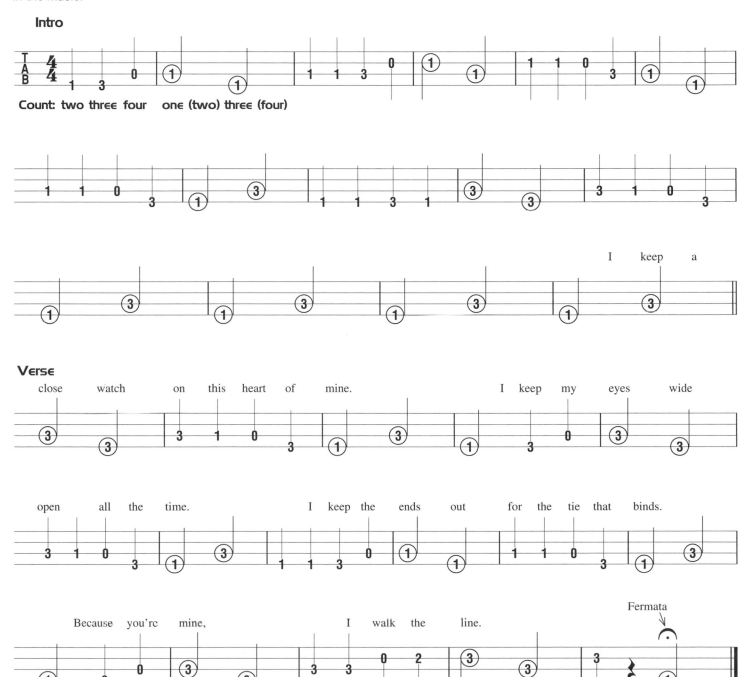

Words and Music by John R. Cash
© 1956 (Renewed 1984) HOUSE OF CASH, INC./Administered by BUG MUSIC, INC., A BMG CHRYSALIS COMPANY
All Rights Reserved   Used by Permission

WIPE OUT 🔊46))

It's time to play your first complete song. "Wipe Out" is one of the most popular instrumental hits of all time. It was originally recorded by the Surfaris in 1963 and has been performed since by numerous groups, including the Ventures and the Beach Boys.

During the famous drum breakdown in the second half of the song, you'll notice a **whole rest**. It indicates one full measure of silence, and looks like this: ▬

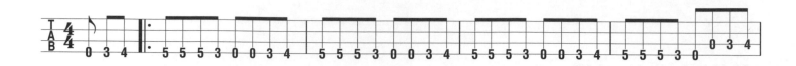

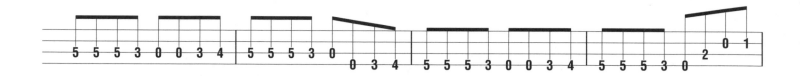

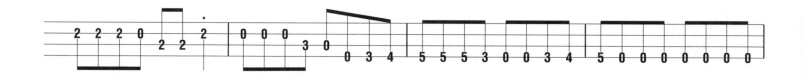

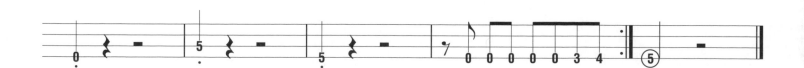

By The Surfaris
© 1963 (Renewed) MIRALESTE MUSIC and ROBIN HOOD MUSIC CO.

THE G STRING

Here are the notes within the first five frets of the 1st string, called the G string.

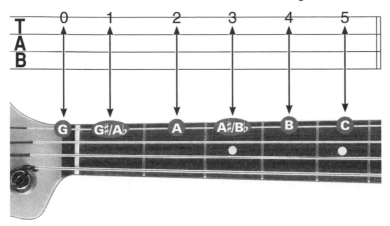

EVERY BREATH YOU TAKE 🔊 47))

Play the melody to this hit pop song by the Police.

Music and Lyrics by Sting
© 1983 G.M. SUMNER
Administered by EMI MUSIC PUBLISHING LIMITED

STAND BY ME 🔊 48))

The bass line to this timeless classic by Ben E. King was originally played on the upright bass, but it sounds just as great on the electric.

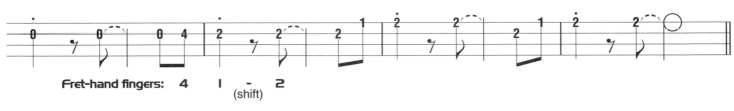

Fret-hand fingers: 4   1   -   2
                            (shift)

Words and Music by Jerry Leiber, Mike Stoller and Ben E. King
Copyright © 1961 Sony/ATV Music Publishing LLC
Copyright Renewed
All Rights Administered by Sony/ATV Music Publishing LLC, 8 Music Square West, Nashville, TN 37203

When a **dot** appears after a note, you extend the note by half its value. A **dotted half note** lasts for three beats.

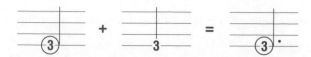

BABA O'RILEY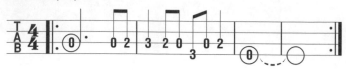

This classic rock riff by the Who has a dotted half note.

Count: one (two - three) four   one (two - three - four)

Words and Music by Peter Townshend
Copyright © 1971 Fabulous Music Ltd.
Copyright Renewed
All Rights in the U.S. and Canada Administered by Spirit One Music o/b/o Spirit Services Holdings, S.à.r.l.,
Suolubaf Music and ABKCO Music, Inc.

THE CHAIN

The famous breakdown in this Fleetwood Mac song features the bass player.

Words and Music by Stevie Nicks, Christine McVie, Lindsey Buckingham, Mick Fleetwood and John McVie
Copyright © 1977 Welsh Witch Music, Universal Music - Careers, Now Sounds Music,
Molly Mac Music and Rattleman Music
Copyright Renewed
All Rights on behalf of Welsh Witch Music Administered by Sony/ATV Music Publishing LLC,
8 Music Square West, Nashville, TN 37203

NORWEGIAN WOOD (THIS BIRD HAS FLOWN)

Play the melody to this Indian-influenced Beatles song in 3/4 time. Here, the dotted half note equals one whole measure.

Words and Music by John Lennon and Paul McCartney
Copyright © 1965 Sony/ATV Music Publishing LLC
Copyright Renewed
All Rights Administered by Sony/ATV Music Publishing LLC, 8 Music Square West, Nashville, TN 37203

RAKE TECHNIQUE

When moving from a high string to a lower one, use the same picking finger to play both strings—this is called the **rake technique**. This will allow you to keep your picking hand relaxed and play with less overall effort. The following examples illustrate when to use your index finger (i) or middle finger (m).

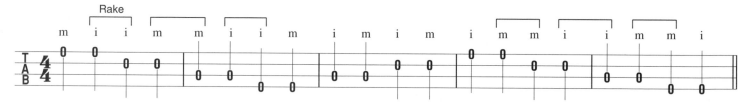

I CAN'T HELP MYSELF (SUGAR PIE, HONEY BUNCH)

This Motown bass line was recorded by the great James Jamerson for the Four Tops. The fingering (rake) pattern reverses every measure.

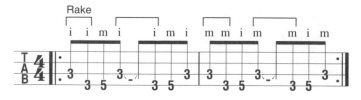

Words and Music by Brian Holland, Lamont Dozier and Edward Holland
© 1965, 1972 (Renewed 1993, 2000) JOBETE MUSIC CO., INC.
All Rights Controlled and Administered by EMI BLACKWOOD MUSIC INC. on behalf of STONE AGATE MUSIC
(A Division of JOBETE MUSIC CO., INC.)

WE GOTTA GET OUT OF THIS PLACE

Use your 1st finger (fret hand) to roll from F down to C in this riff by the Animals. The roll should be executed starting with the pad of your finger on F and moving toward the tip for C.

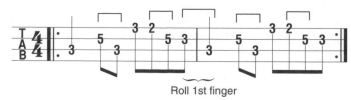

Roll 1st finger

Words and Music by Barry Mann and Cynthia Weil
© 1965 (Renewed 1993) SCREEN GEMS-EMI MUSIC INC.

CHECKPOINT

You're halfway through this book and well on your way to a rewarding hobby or a successful career with the electric bass guitar. Let's take a moment to review some of what you've learned so far.

NOTE NAMES

Draw a line to match each note on the left with its correct name on the right.

```
T
A 2
B
```
C

```
T
A 1
B
```
B

```
T   2
A
B
```
G

```
T
A 3
B
```
E

```
T
A   0
B
```
F

```
T
A
B   3
```
A

```
T
A
B 0
```
D

SYMBOLS & TERMS

Draw a line to match each symbol on the left with its correct name on the right.

𝄽   Time Signature

3/4   Half Note

(repeat sign)   Eighth Rest

𝅗𝅥   Quarter Rest

—   Eighth Note

𝄾   Repeat Sign

♪   Half Rest

Write the note names in the spaces provided.

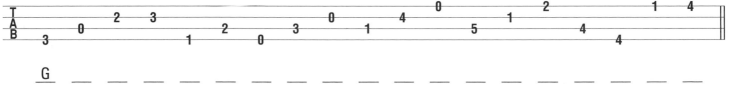

G _ _ _ _ _ _ _ _ _ _ _ _ _ _ _ _ _ _ _

Add bar lines.

Below the tab staff are note names. Write the notes on the tab staff.

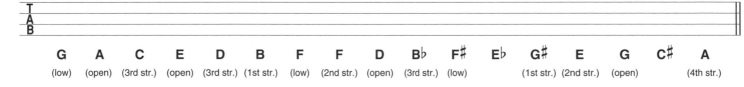

G	A	C	E	D	B	F	F	D	B♭	F♯	E♭	G♯	E	G	C♯	A
(low)	(open)	(3rd str.)	(open)	(3rd str.)	(1st str.)	(low)	(2nd str.)	(open)	(3rd str.)	(low)		(1st str.)	(2nd str.)	(open)		(4th str.)

SIGNED, SEALED, DELIVERED I'M YOURS 54))

This Stevie Wonder song features a bass line by legendary bassist James Jamerson. The verse section is tabbed with **ending brackets**. On the first time through, play the 1st ending and repeat back to the beginning of the verse. The second time, skip the 1st ending and play the 2nd ending.

Intro

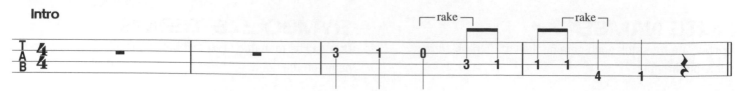

Verse

1. Like a fool I went and stayed too long.   Now I'm wonderin' if your love's
2. Then that time I went and said goodbye.   Now I'm back and not ashamed

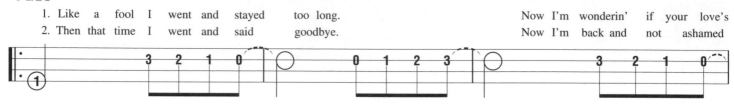

still strong.   Oo,   baby,   here I am,   signed, sealed, delivered,   I'm yours.
to cry.

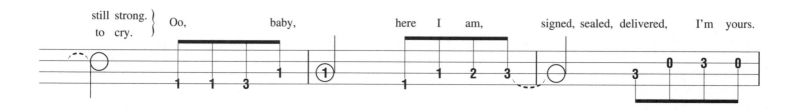

1.   2.   Here I am

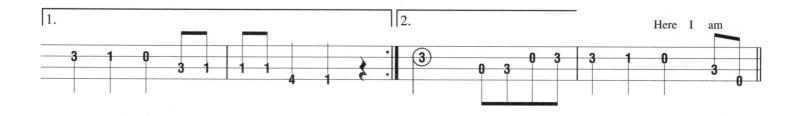

Chorus

baby,   signed, sealed, delivered,   I'm yours.   Here I am

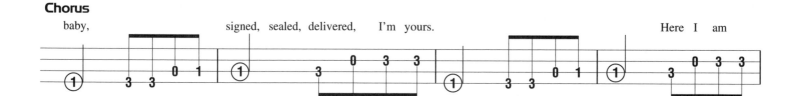

baby,   signed, sealed, delivered, I'm yours.

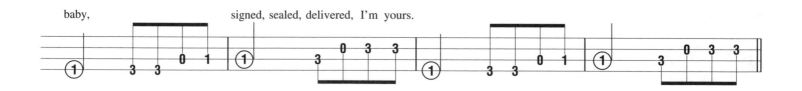

Outro

Words and Music by Stevie Wonder, Syreeta Wright, Lee Garrett and Lula Mae Hardaway
© 1970 (Renewed 1998) JOBETE MUSIC CO., INC., BLACK BULL MUSIC and SAWANDI MUSIC
c/o EMI APRIL MUSIC INC. and EMI BLACKWOOD MUSIC INC.

PLAYING WITH A PICK

A pick produces a clear, distinct sound, and is a popular choice for rock bass. Some of rock's greatest bassists like Paul McCartney (The Beatles), Chris Squire (Yes), and Krist Novoselic (Nirvana) use a pick almost exclusively, while many others switch between pick and fingerstyle.

Picks come in various thicknesses. For the bass, a medium to heavy gauge pick will give you the best tone. To hold it properly, first curl your index finger and place the pick on top with the tip sticking out. Then place your thumb over the top of the pick and hold it firmly. There should be about 3/8 inch of the tip extending out. Place the flat side of the pick against the string, and drag the pick across.

You can pick with either downstrokes (⊓) or upstrokes (V). Downstrokes produce a stronger sound, but upstrokes are used in conjunction with downstrokes when playing faster bass lines, or when the specific sound of alternating strokes is required for a song.

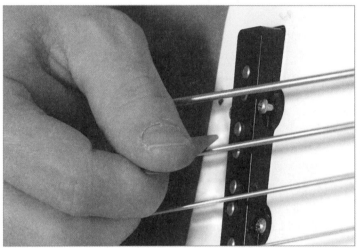

Downstroke

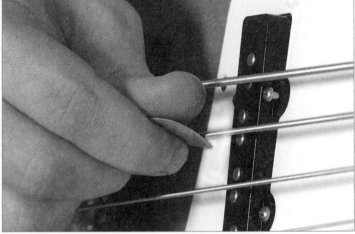

Upstroke

ADAM'S SONG 🔊55))

Try picking with all downstrokes on this Blink-182 bass line the first few times. Afterwards, play it again with alternating strokes (down-up-down-up) to feel and hear the difference.

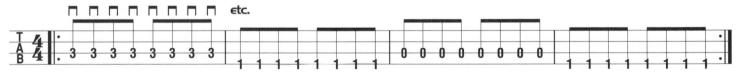

Words and Music by Tom De Longe and Mark Hoppus
© 1999 EMI APRIL MUSIC INC. and FUN WITH GOATS
All Rights Controlled and Administered by EMI APRIL MUSIC INC.

VERTIGO 🔊56))

This U2 song has a bass part that's a little tricky. Always begin slowly when playing a new song and gradually work it up to speed.

COME AS YOU ARE 🔊57))

The last two song examples were driving, rock bass lines that sound good picked with all downstrokes. This riff by Nirvana, by contrast, requires a looser feel that can be achieved with alternate picking. As a general rule, upstrokes are used on the "and" of beats as noted here.

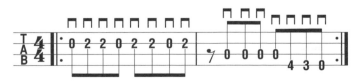

Words by Bono and The Edge
Music by U2
Copyright © 2004 UNIVERSAL MUSIC PUBLISHING INTERNATIONAL B.V.
All Rights in the United States and Canada Controlled and Administered by UNIVERSAL - POLYGRAM INTERNATIONAL
PUBLISHING, INC.

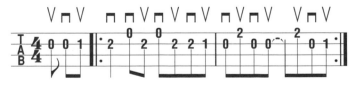

Words and Music by Kurt Cobain
© 1991 THE END OF MUSIC and PRIMARY WAVE TUNES
All Rights Controlled and Administered by EMI VIRGIN SONGS, INC.

ROXANNE 🔊 58))

Sting, the bassist and singer of the band the Police, used a pick on the song "Roxanne." You can play the bass lines to the intro, verse, and pre-chorus with all downstrokes to get a strong, even sound. Then switch to alternate picking for the eighth notes leading into the chorus.

Once you reach the end of the interlude section on the second page, you'll see the instructions "D.S. al Coda." Jump back to the sign (𝄋) at the beginning of the verse and play up to the instruction "To Coda." At this point, skip to the last line of the tune that is labeled "Coda," and play the final four measures.

Intro

The sign
↓
𝄋 **Verse**

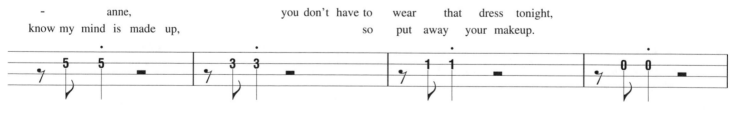

Music and Lyrics by Sting
© 1978 G.M. SUMNER
Administered by EMI MUSIC PUBLISHING LIMITED

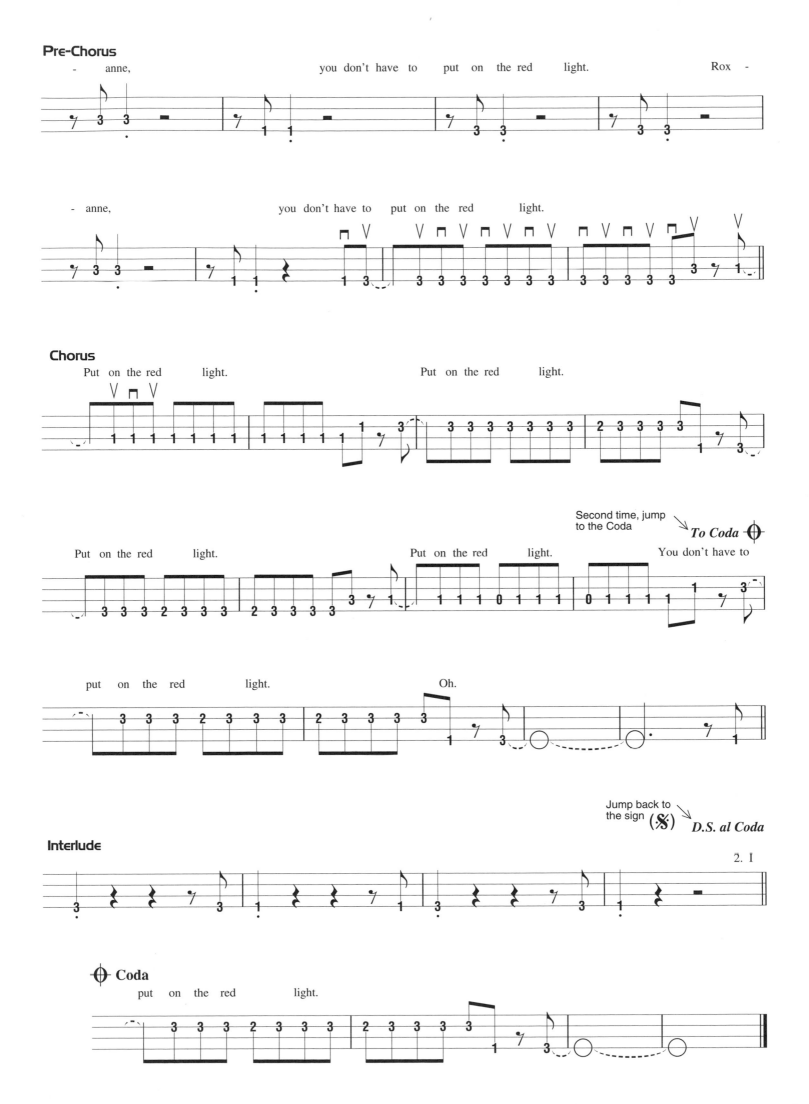

THE MUSICAL ALPHABET AND OCTAVES

The basic musical alphabet consists of seven notes—A through G. This series of notes repeats as you extend beyond G at the top or descend beyond A below.

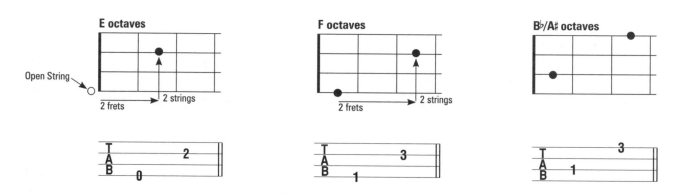

The distance from any one note to the same note up or down eight letters in the musical alphabet is called an **octave**. The two notes of the octave will share the same letter name and sound very much alike, except one will be higher and the other lower in pitch.

Octaves follow a movable pattern on the fretboard. To find an octave above any note on the E or A string, move up two frets and across two strings as illustrated below.

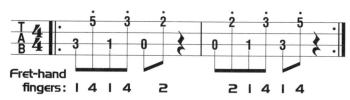

LOVE ROLLERCOASTER 59

This song was a #1 hit for funk group the Ohio Players and was later covered by the Red Hot Chili Peppers. Follow the indicated fret-hand fingerings and alternate your picking fingers. Pluck the lower notes with your index finger and the higher octave notes with your middle finger.

Words and Music by Ralph Middlebrooks, James Williams, Marshall Jones, Leroy Bonner, Clarence Satchell, William Beck and Marvin Pierce
© 1975 (Renewed 2003) SEGUNDO SUENOS (BMI)/Administered by BUG MUSIC, INC., A BMG CHRYSALIS COMPANY and RICK'S MUSIC INC. (BMI)/Administered by RIGHTSONG MUSIC INC.

MY SHARONA 60

On the repeat of this riff by the Knack, fret the low F♯ with your 1st finger. Then shift your hand up one fret to begin again at G with the same finger.

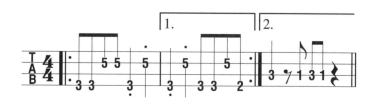

Words and Music by Doug Fieger and Berton Averre
Copyright © 1979 by Three Wise Boys Music, LLC (BMI), Small Hill Music (ASCAP) and Eighties Music (ASCAP)
All Rights for Small Hill Music and Eighties Music Controlled and Administered by Hi Pitch Music Services

SMOKE ON THE WATER 61

The verse section of this legendary rock song consists of mostly G and F octave notes.

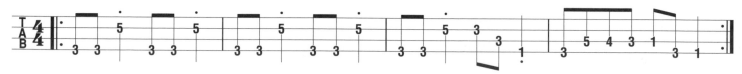

Words and Music by Ritchie Blackmore, Ian Gillan, Roger Glover, Jon Lord and Ian Paice
© 1972 (Renewed 2000) B. FELDMAN & CO. LTD. trading as HEC MUSIC
All Rights for the United States and Canada Controlled and Administered by GLENWOOD MUSIC CORP.

THE BOX SHAPE

The **box shape** is a four-note, moveable pattern on the fretboard that can be found in bass lines of all styles. The lowest note in the pattern is called the **root note**, and the highest is the octave. The root note got its name because it serves as the strongest note of the group from which everything else is based.

Below are illustrations of the box shape on the fretboard in a few different positions.

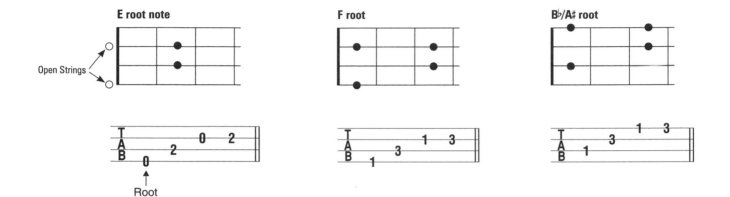

PUNCHING BAG 🔊62))

This bass line starts on the root note A and is a great practice for the rake technique if using your fingers.

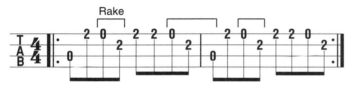

Copyright © 2013 by HAL LEONARD CORPORATION

NIGHT TRAIN 🔊63))

Follow the correct fret-hand fingering on this James Brown bass riff to minimize hand stress.

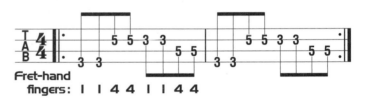

Words by Oscar Washington and Lewis C. Simpkins
Music by Jimmy Forrest
Copyright © 1952 (Renewed) by Embassy Music Corporation (BMI)

WHAT'D I SAY 🔊64))

The box shape can often be found in blues songs like this classic by Ray Charles. "What'd I Say" is an example of a twelve-measure, repeating song form called a **12-bar blues**.

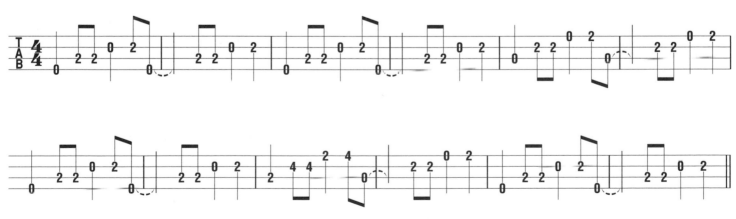

Words and Music by Ray Charles
© 1959, 1960 (Renewed) UNICHAPPELL MUSIC, INC. and MIJAC MUSIC
All Rights for MIJAC MUSIC Administered by SONY/ATV MUSIC PUBLISHING LLC, 8 Music Square West, Nashville, TN 37203

BLACK MAGIC WOMAN 🔊 65))

The box shape can be played anywhere on the neck of the bass. For this song made famous by Santana, we're moving a little beyond the notes we have learned so far to illustrate this idea.

In any song, the bass line corresponds directly to **chords** that a guitarist or pianist plays. These chords are notated with **chord symbols** found above the staff. Notice that the root note of the box shape moves along with the changing chords.

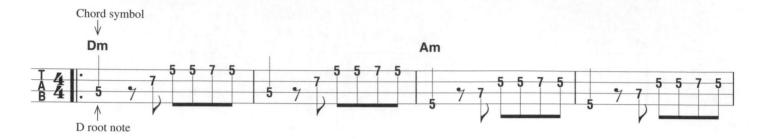

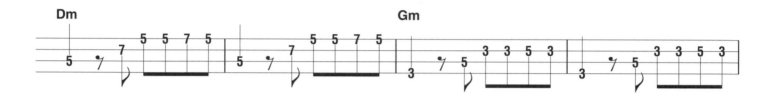

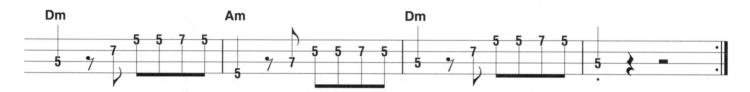

Words and Music by Peter Green
© Copyright 1968 and 1970 by King Publishing Co. Ltd., London, England
Copyright Renewed
Worldwide Rights Assigned to Bourne Music Ltd.
All Rights for the U.S.A. and Canada Controlled by Murbo Music Publishing Inc. (BMI)

JUMPIN' AND JIVIN' 🔊 66))

Here is one more example of a 12-bar blues. This one goes beyond the box shape by adding some outside notes to the mix, but it's a must-know, standard bass line that has been used in countless jazz, blues, and rockabilly songs.

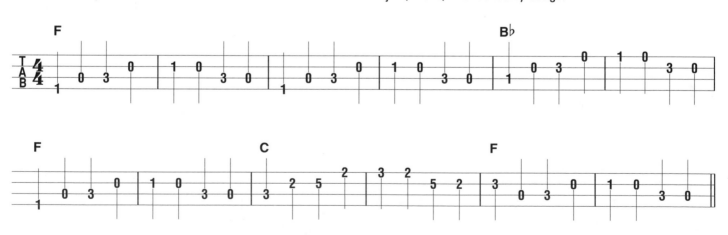

Copyright © 2013 by HAL LEONARD CORPORATION

MORE RHYTHMS

You've already learned that a dot after a note increases the value by one half. Therefore a **dotted quarter note** lasts for 1-1/2 beats.

A very common bass rhythm that incorporates the dotted quarter note is shown below. For counting, it can be helpful to think of a dotted quarter note as a quarter tied to an eighth.

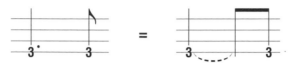

RIKKI DON'T LOSE THAT NUMBER 67

A latin-inspired bass line serves as an introduction to this Steely Dan song.

Count: one (two) and three (four) and

Words and Music by Walter Becker and Donald Fagen
Copyright © 1974 UNIVERSAL MUSIC CORP.
Copyright Renewed

DEVILS HAIRCUT 68

This song by Beck can be played with a finger roll across all three strings.

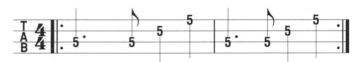

Count: one (two) and three four

Words and Music by John King, Michael Simpson, Beck Hansen, James Brown, Philip Coulter and Tommy Scott
Copyright © 1996 UNIVERSAL MUSIC CORP., DUST BROTHERS MUSIC, CYANIDE BREATHMINT MUSIC, TRIO MUSIC, FORT KNOX MUSIC, INC. and PHILIP R. SOLOMON MUSIC
All Rights for DUST BROTHERS MUSIC Controlled and Administered by UNIVERSAL MUSIC CORP.
All Rights for CYANIDE BREATHMINT MUSIC Administered by KOBALT MUSIC PUBLISHING AMERICA, INC.
All Rights for TRIO MUSIC Administered by BUG MUSIC, INC. a BMG CHRYSALIS COMPANY
Embodies portions of "Out Of Sight" written by James Brown, © 1965 (Renewed) by Freddy Bienstock Music Co.
(administered by Fort Knox Music, Inc.), controlled by Fort Knox Music, Inc. and Trio Music for the world excluding the
United States; and "I Can Only Give You Everything" written by Philip Coulter and Tommy Scott, © 1966 (Renewed) by
Carlin Music Corp. (administered in the U.S. and Canada by Carbert Music Inc.)

WEREWOLVES OF LONDON 69

The rhythm from the last two examples is reversed here.

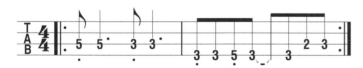

Words and Music by Warren Zevon, Robert Wachtel and LeRoy Marinel
© 1978, 1979 EMI VIRGIN MUSIC LTD. and TINY TUNES MUSIC
All Rights for EMI VIRGIN MUSIC LTD. Controlled and Administered by EMI VIRGIN SONGS, INC.
All Rights for TINY TUNES MUSIC Administered by MUSIC & MEDIA INTERNATIONAL, INC.

THE END 70

As made famous by Duke Ellington, this short riff is a standard ending to a lot of songs.

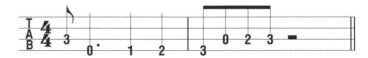

Copyright © 2013 by HAL LEONARD CORPORATION

FEEL GOOD INC 71

Here's a song by Gorillaz that ties a dotted quarter note to a half note.

Words and Music by Damon Albarn, Jamie Hewlett, Brian Burton and De La Soul
© 2005 GORILLAZ, UNDERGROUND ANIMALS and 80'S KID MUSIC
All Rights for GORILLAZ in the U.S. and Canada Controlled and Administered by EMI BLACKWOOD MUSIC INC.

OH, PRETTY WOMAN 72

Sometimes the time signature, or **meter**, can change within a song as it does in this one by Roy Orbison. A measure of 2/4 time has two beats, and a quarter note receives one beat. The meter changes in this song happen for only one measure before changing back to 4/4, so count aloud to help get through those passages.

Verse

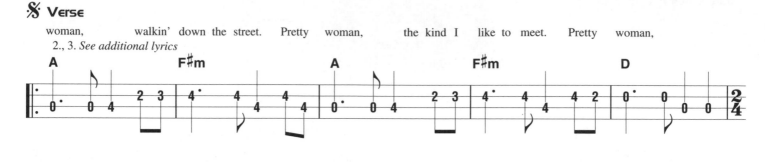

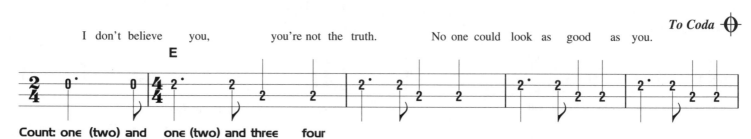

Count: one (two) and one (two) and three   four

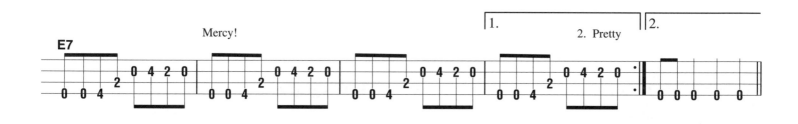

Bridge

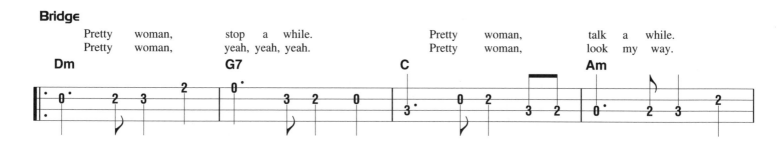

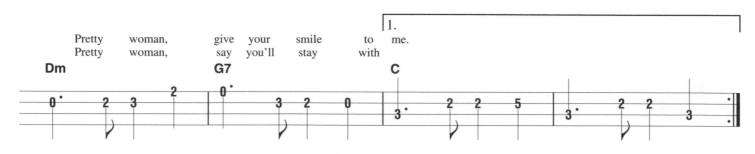

Words and Music by Roy Orbison and Bill Dees

Copyright © 1964 (Renewed 1992) ROY ORBISON MUSIC COMPANY, BARBARA ORBISON MUSIC COMPANY and SONY/ATV MUSIC PUBLISHING LLC
All Rights on behalf of ROY ORBISON MUSIC COMPANY and BARBARA ORBISON MUSIC COMPANY Administered by BMG RIGHTS MANAGEMENT (US) LLC
All Rights on behalf of SONY/ATV MUSIC PUBLISHING LLC Administered by SONY/ATV MUSIC PUBLISHING LLC, 8 Music Square West, Nashville, TN 37203

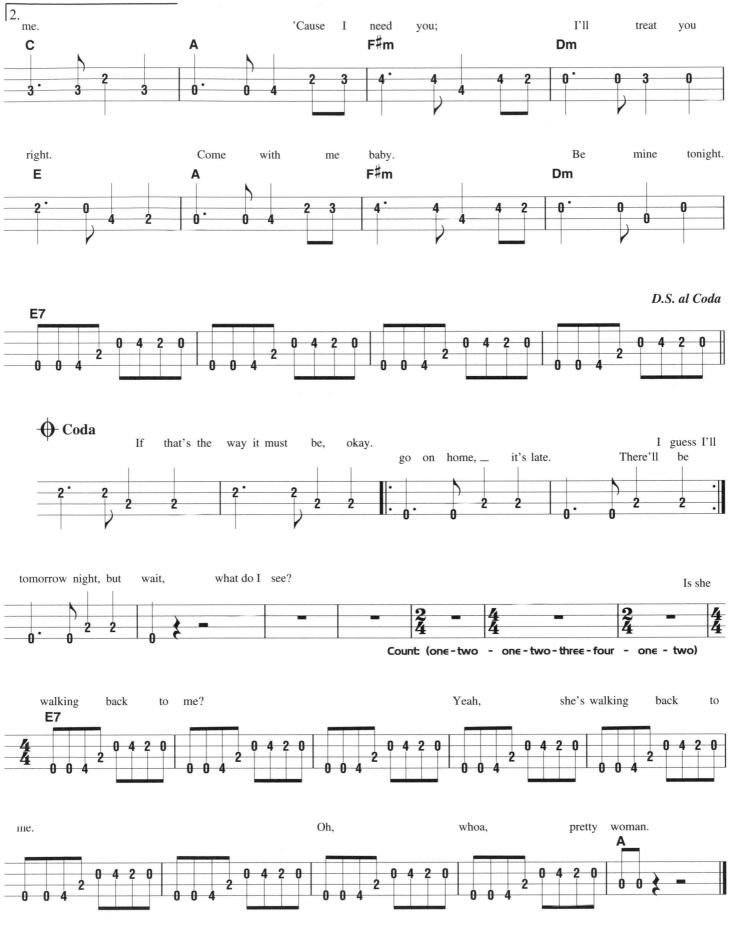

Additional Lyrics

2. Pretty woman, won't you pardon me?
Pretty woman, I couldn't help but see;
Pretty woman, that you look lovely as can be.
Are you lonely just like me?

3. Pretty woman, don't walk on by.
Pretty woman, don't make me cry.
Pretty woman, don't walk away.
Okay.

SYNCOPATION

Syncopation is the placement of rhythmic accents on weak beats or on weak portions of beats. Syncopated eighth notes emphasize the upbeat, or "and" of a beat.

The eighth–quarter–eighth rhythm shown here is found in all styles of music. What makes this rhythm a little tricky is that the quarter note starts on an upbeat. To help, count the quarter note as if it is two tied eighth notes as illustrated below.

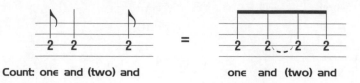

Count: one and (two) and   one and (two) and

RADAR LOVE 73))

This driving rock song by Golden Earring features a picked bass intro, but it can also be played fingerstyle.

Words and Music by George Kooymans and Barry Hay
Copyright © 1973 Snamyook
Copyright Renewed
All Rights Administered by Sony/ATV Music Publishing LLC, 8 Music Square West, Nashville, TN 37203

GREEN ACRES THEME 74))

The classic TV show "Green Acres" used this tune as a theme.

Music and Lyrics by Vic Mizzy
Copyright © 1965, Renewed 1993 by Unison Music Company (ASCAP)
Administered by Next Decade Entertainment, Inc.

PROUD MARY 75))

In the first and second measures of this song recorded by Creedence Clearwater Revival, there are accents on the "and" of beat 2. The third measure, however, contains the most syncopated part of the whole intro with accents on the "and" of beats 2, 3, and 4.

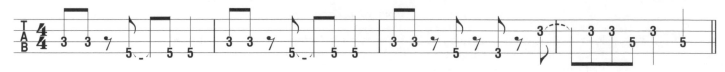

Words and Music by John Fogerty
Copyright © 1968 Jondora Music
Copyright Renewed

MUSTANG SALLY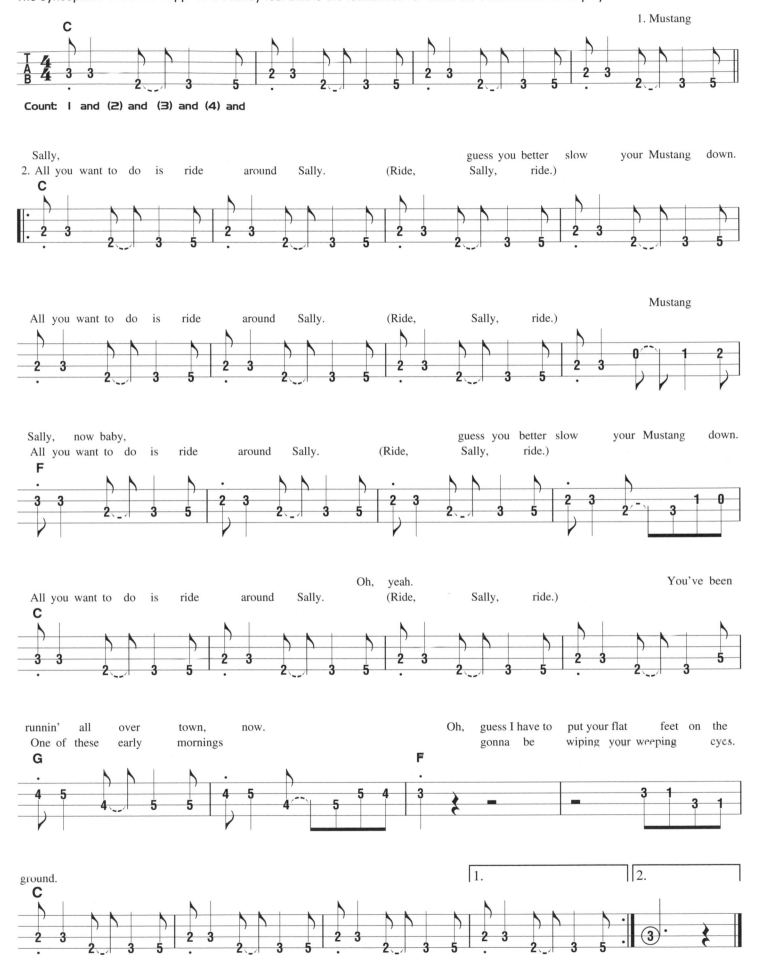

Many artists have recorded this song through the years, but Wilson Pickett's version has become a timeless soul classic. The syncopated bass line supplies a bouncy feel that is the foundation for what the other instruments play.

Words and Music by Bonny Rice
Copyright © 1965 Fourteenth Hour Music, Inc.
Copyright Renewed

SLIDES, HAMMER-ONS & PULL-OFFS

Sometimes, it's not so much what you play, it's how you play it. In music terms, this is called **articulation**. Slides, hammer-ons, and pull-offs all belong to a special category of articulations called **legato**. Legato techniques allow you to connect two or more consecutive notes together to create a smooth, flowing sound.

To play a **slide**, pick the first note as you normally would. Then, maintain pressure as you move your fret-hand finger up or down the fretboard to sound the second note. (The second note is not picked.) In tab, a slide is indicated with a short, slanted line and a curved **slur**.

SWEET LEAF

Here is a classic heavy metal riff by the band Black Sabbath. Execute the first slide from D to D♭ with your 2nd finger. That will set you up to play C with your 1st finger.

Words and Music by Frank Iommi, John Osbourne, William Ward and Terence Butler
© Copyright 1971 (Renewed) and 1974 (Renewed) Westminster Music Ltd., London, England
TRO - Essex Music International, Inc., New York, controls all publication rights for the U.S.A. and Canada

THE BEETLE

If this bass line sounds familiar, it's because there are many recorded variations of it throughout popular music. Use your 4th finger to execute both slides in this example.

Copyright © 2013 by HAL LEONARD CORPORATION

THE MUNSTERS THEME (79))

Beginning in measure 3, slide from F to F♯ with your 3rd finger and play the top note (B on the G string) with your 4th in this TV theme song.

By Jack Marshall
Copyright © 1973 SONGS OF UNIVERSAL, INC.
Copyright Renewed

To play a **hammer-on**, pluck the first note and then press down, or "hammer on" to, a higher note along the same string. The initial attack should carry over to produce sound from the second note without picking again. If the first note is fretted, it helps to keep the first note held down when executing the hammer-on.

In tab, a hammer-on is notated with a curved slur connecting two notes.

MOUNTAIN SONG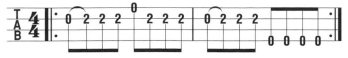

This Jane's Addiction song features a cool bass line with a couple hammer-ons on the D string.

Words and Music by Jane's Addiction
Copyright © 1988 I'LL HIT YOU BACK MUSIC, EMBRYOTIC MUSIC, SWIZZLESTICK MUSIC and BUBBLY ORANGE STUFF MUSIC
All Rights for I'LL HIT YOU BACK MUSIC, EMBRYOTIC MUSIC and SWIZZLESTICK MUSIC Controlled and Administered by IRVING MUSIC, INC.
All Rights for BUBBLY ORANGE STUFF MUSIC Controlled and Administered by EMI BLACKWOOD MUSIC INC.

TAXATION

Here's an ode to a famous bass line that uses the box shape.

Copyright © 2013 by HAL LEONARD CORPORATION

BRING IT ON HOME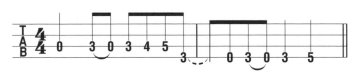

The **grace-note slide** on the "and" of beat 4 in this Led Zeppelin riff denotes a very quick slide to the primary (second) note.

Written by Willie Dixon
© 1964 (Renewed 1992) HOOCHIE COOCHIE MUSIC (BMI)/Administered by BUG MUSIC, INC., a BMG CHRYSALIS company

LOW RIDER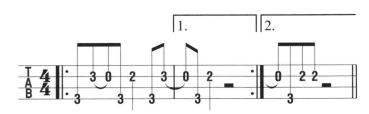

The bass riff to "Low Rider" may be one of the most recognizable in rock music. Keep your 1st finger planted through both hammer-ons.

Fret-hand fingers: 1 4   1   4   4   1   4 1 4 1 4

Words and Music by Sylvester Allen, Harold R. Brown, Morris Dickerson, Jerry Goldstein, Leroy Jordan, Lee Oskar, Charles W. Miller and Howard Scott
Copyright © 1975 FAR OUT MUSIC, INC.
Copyright Renewed
All Rights Controlled and Administered by BMG RIGHTS MANAGEMENT (US) LLC
All Rights Reserved Used by Permission

A **pull-off** is the opposite of a hammer-on. It is the technique used to slur from a higher note to a lower one. Start with your finger planted on the first note of the slur. Pluck the higher note and then tug, or "pull," that finger off the string to sound the lower note.

LEAD BALLOON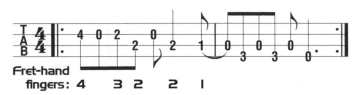

It's a common mistake when attempting a pull-off to pull the string out of tune before the release. This is usually the result of simply pulling too hard.

Copyright © 2013 by HAL LEONARD CORPORATION

CULT OF PERSONALITY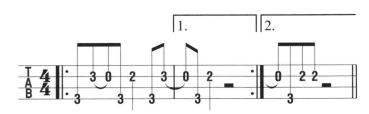

Start with your 2nd finger on G and use your 3rd finger to execute the pull-off for this riff by Living Colour.

Words and Music by William Calhoun, Corey Glover, Muzz Skillings and Vernon Reid
Copyright © 1988 Sony/ATV Music Publishing LLC, Dare To Dream Music, Darkology Music, Teenage Dog Music and Muzz Skillings Designee
All Rights Administered by Sony/ATV Music Publishing LLC, 8 Music Square West, Nashville, TN 37203

LOVE IN AN ELEVATOR

This is the intro riff to one of Aerosmith's biggest hits. The fingering below will help set you up for the pull-off on the A string.

Fret-hand fingers: 4   3 2   2   1

Words and Music by Tyler/Perry
© 1989 EMI APRIL MUSIC INC., JUJU RHYTHMS and PRIMARY WAVE STEVEN TYLER
All Rights for JUJU RHYTHMS Controlled and Administered by EMI APRIL MUSIC INC.

RAIN

You can combine legato articulations as this Beatles bass line demonstrates. The last three notes in measure 2 meld a hammer-on and pull-off in one continuous motion. Keep your 1st finger planted on the F through the entire hammer-on/pull-off combination.

Words and Music by John Lennon and Paul McCartney
Copyright © 1966 Sony/ATV Music Publishing LLC
Copyright Renewed
All Rights Administered by Sony/ATV Music Publishing LLC, 8 Music Square West, Nashville, TN 37203

OTHERSIDE 88))

What better way to wrap up this book than with one of the Red Hot Chili Peppers' biggest hits. The bass line to "Otherside" contains slides, hammer-ons, syncopated rhythms, and more!

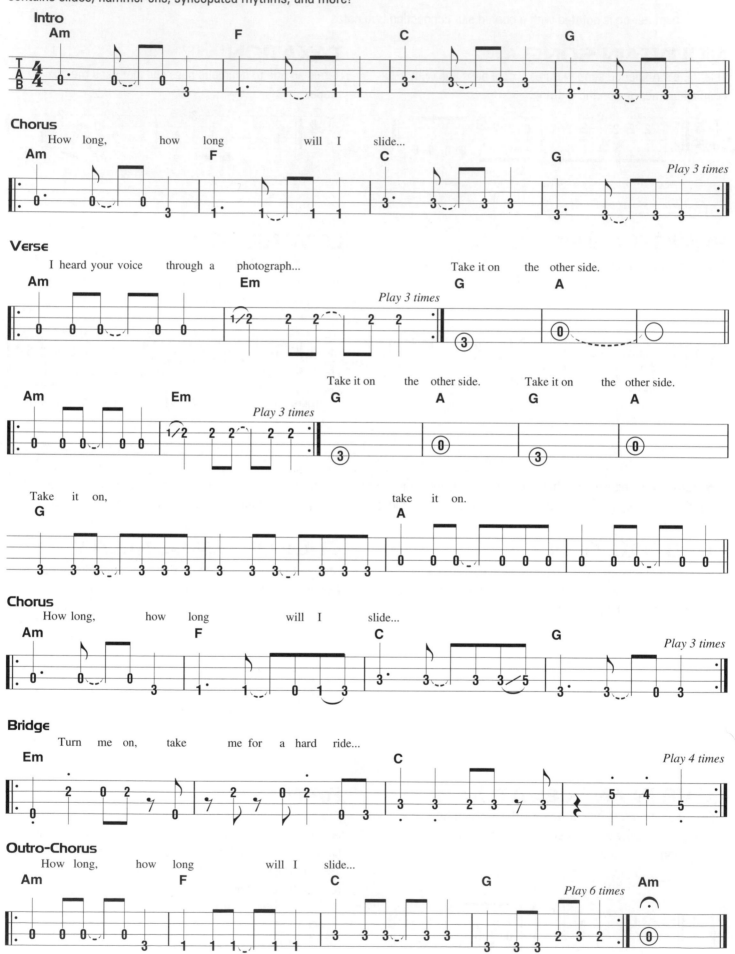

Words and Music by Anthony Kiedis, Flea, John Frusciante and Chad Smith
© 1999 MOEBETOBLAME MUSIC